THE GODS AND THE WORLD

SALLUST
ON
THE GODS
AND
THE WORLD

AND THE
PYTHAGORIC SENTENCES
OF
DEMOPHILUS

AND
FIVE HYMNS BY PROCLUS

TRANSLATED FROM THE GREEK BY
THOMAS TAYLOR

Originally published in London, 1793.

The layout, design, and cover art of this edition copyright © 2017 Strigoi Publishing.

ISBN-13: 978-1974272051
ISBN-10: 1974272052

PREFACE

THE present volume contains three pieces of composition, each of which, though inconsiderable as to its bulk, is inestimable as to the value of its contents. The first of these is the production of Sallust, a Platonic philosopher, who is considered by Gale as the same Sallust that, according to Suidas, was contemporary with Proclus, and who appears to have been alive when Simplicius wrote his Commentaries on Epictetus: but though the testimony of Suidas, or rather Damascius, from whose History of Philosophers Suidas derived his account of Sallust, is very decisive as to the existence of a philosopher of this name, yet there are two particulars which, in my opinion, render it very doubtful whether the author of the present treatise is the Sallust mentioned by Suidas. The first is, that the Sallust of Suidas is said to have asserted, "that it was not easy, but rather impossible, for men to philosophize;" an assertion, as Damascius well observes, which is neither true, nor worthy to be uttered, and which is certainly very inconsistent with what the author of the present treatise asserts: for (in Chap. XIII.) he informs us, that his book was composed for that class of mankind whose souls may be considered as neither incurable, nor yet capable of being elevated by philosophy; plainly acknowledging by this, that some men are capable of philosophizing in a proper manner, and thus evidently contradicting the dogma of the Sallust mentioned by Damascius and Suidas. But there is another particular which militates against this opinion, and which is of no less weight than that we have just now mentioned; and this is, the disagreement which is related by Suidas to have taken place between Sallust and Proclus; for the author of the following book, as was obvious to the learned philologist Gale, treads every where in the footsteps of Proclus: not to mention that the Sallust of Suidas, by composing Orations after the manner of the ancients, and philosophizing like the Cynics, can hardly be supposed to be that *profound* philosopher who wrote the ensuing treatise *On the Gods and the World*.

It is, however, sufficient for our purpose, that the work itself is fortunately preserved entire, whatever uncertainty we may labour under concerning its real author; I say fortunately preserved, for it may be considered as a beautiful epitome of the Platonic philosophy, in which the most important dogmas are delivered with such elegant conciseness, perfect accuracy, and strength of argument, that it is difficult to say to which the treatise is most entitled—our admiration or our praise. I have before observed, that this little work was composed by its author with a view of benefiting a middle class of mankind, whose souls are neither incurable, nor yet capable of ascending through philosophy to the summit of human attainments: but in order to understand this distinction properly, it is necessary to inform the reader, that human souls may be distributed into three ranks; into such as live a life pure and impassive when compared with the multitude; into such as are neither wholly pure nor yet perfectly impure; and into such as are profoundly impure. Souls of the first class, which are consequently the fewest in number, may be called divine souls, heroes and demi-gods, and when invested with a terrene body, form such men as Pythagoras, Plato, Plotinus, Jamblichus, Proclus, &c., were of old: souls of this kind, not only descend into mortality in consequence of that necessity by which all human souls are at times drawn down to the earth, but for the benevolent purpose of benefiting such as are of an inferior class; they likewise easily recover a remembrance of their pristine state, and, in consequence of this, descend no farther than to the earth. But souls of the middle class, for whom the book of Sallust is designed, in consequence of becoming vitiated and defiled, though not in an incurable degree, are incapable of acquiring in the present life philosophic perfection and purity, and are with great difficulty, and even scarcely able to ascend, after long periods, to the beatific vision of the intelligible world. But souls of the third class, are such as, from their profound impurity, and from having drank immoderately deep of oblivion, may be considered as abiding perpetually in life, as in the dark regions of Tartarus, from which, through having lost all freedom of the will, they can never emerge.

But we may easily collect the propriety of this distribution, by considering, that there must necessarily be two mediums between souls that abide on high with purity, such as the souls of *essential* heroes, who are perpetual attendants on the gods, and souls that descend with the greatest impurity; and these mediums can be no other than souls that descend indeed, but with purity, and souls that descend, and are partly pure and partly impure.

With respect to the sentences of Demophilus, which are the next in order, I have only to observe, that we know nothing more of the author than that he was most probably a Pythagorian, and that he collected these sentences from the works of more ancient Pythagoreans, by whom they were employed like proverbs, on account of their intrinsic excellence and truth. The same person, too, is the author of another little piece called *Similitudes*, of which I may probably, at some future period, publish a translation.

As to the five hymns of Proclus, they are unfortunately nothing more than the wreck of a great multitude which were composed by this admirable man; and the last of these was first discovered by me among the Harleian MSS. in the British Museum, and published in my Dissertation on the Eleusinian and Bacchic Mysteries. Of the life of Proclus by Marinus, I have long since given a translation, to which I refer the reader for an account of this incomparable man. I only add, that the four first hymns are justly admired by all the critics as most beautiful pieces of composition; and they would doubtless have passed the same judgment on the fifth, had it been extant for their perusal.

In the last place, the reader will find five hymns of my own composing, and which form only a part of a complete collection to all the divinities, which I design to publish at some future and more auspicious period than they present. My principal intention with regard to the public in the composition of most of these hymns was, to elucidate the ancient Theology, by explaining the mystic appellations of the gods: but my design with respect to myself was to reap that most solid advantage with which the celebration of divinity *in a becoming manner* is invariably attended. The author from whom this explanation is principally derived is Proclus; and those conceptions, which may properly be considered as my own, will, I hope, be found consistent with the doctrines of Plato and his genuine disciples. In many parts likewise of the hymn to Jupiter, I acknowledge myself greatly indebted to the elegant hymns of

Synesius, which I should have translated long since, had they not been so replete with a certain horrid and gigantic impiety, which not only eradicates from the soul that most natural conception, that there are gods subordinate to the first cause, but introduces the most dire of all opinions in its stead, that a mere mortal is equal to the highest god!

TABLE OF CONTENTS

PREFACE v

SALLUST ON THE GODS AND THE WORLD 15

THE PYTHAGORIC SENTENCES OF DEMOPHILUS 53

FIVE HYMNS BY PROCLUS 61

HYMNS BY THE TRANSLATOR 75

SALLUST
ON THE
GODS
AND THE
WORLD

SALLUST
ON THE
GODS
AND THE
WORLD

CHAPTER I

What the Requisites are which an Auditor concerning the Gods ought to possess: and of common Conceptions.

IT is requisite that those who are willing to hear concerning the gods should have been well informed from their childhood, and not nourished with foolish opinions. It is likewise necessary that they should be naturally prudent and good, that they may receive, and properly understand, the discourses which they hear. The knowledge likewise of common conceptions is necessary; but common conceptions are such things as all men, when interrogated, acknowledge to be indubitably certain; such as, that every god is good, without passivity, and free from all mutation; for every thing which is changed, is either changed into something better or into something worse: and if into something worse, it will become depraved, but if into something better, it must have been evil in the beginning.

CHAPTER II

That a God is immutable, without Generation, eternal, incorporeal, and has no Subsistence in Place.

AND such are the requisites for an auditor of the gods. But the necessary discourses proceed as follows: the essences of the gods are neither generated; for eternal natures are without generation; and those beings are eternal who possess a first power, and are naturally void of passivity. Nor are their essences composed from bodies; for even the powers of bodies are incorporeal: nor are they comprehended in place; for this is the property of bodies: nor are they separated from the first cause, or from each other*; in the same manner as intellections are not separated from intellect, nor sciences from the soul.

---

* The reader must not suppose from this, that the gods are nothing more than so many attributes of the first cause; for if this were the case, the first god would be multitude, but *the one* must always be prior to *the many*. But the gods, though they are profoundly united with their ineffable cause, are at the same time *self-perfect* essences; for the first cause is prior to *self-perfection*. Hence as the first cause is superessential, all the gods, from their union through the summits or blossoms of their natures with this incomprehensible god, will be likewise superessential; in the same manner as trees from being rooted in the earth are all of them earthly in an eminent degree. And as in this instance the earth itself is essentially distinct from the trees which it contains, so the highest god is transcendentally distinct from the multitude of gods which he ineffably comprehends.

CHAPTER III

*Concerning Fables, that these are divine,
and on what Account they are so.*

ON what account then the ancients, neglecting such discourses as these, employed fables, is a question not unworthy our investigation. And this indeed is the first utility arising from fables, that they excite us to inquiry, and do not suffer our cogitative power to remain in indolent rest. It will not be difficult therefore to shew that fables are divine, from those by whom they are employed: for they are used by poets agitated by divinity, by the best of philosophers, and by such as disclose initiatory rites. In oracles also fables are employed by the gods; but why fables are divine is the part of philosophy to investigate. Since therefore all beings rejoice in similitude, and are averse from dissimilitude, it is necessary that discourses concerning the gods should be as similar to them as possible, that they may become worthy of their essence, and that they may render the gods propitious to those who discourse concerning them; all which can only be effected by fables. Fables therefore imitate the gods, according to effable and ineffable, unapparent and apparent, wise and ignorant; and this likewise extends to the goodness of the gods; for as the gods impart the goods of sensible natures in common to all things, but the goods resulting from intelligibles to the wise alone, so fables assert to all men that there are gods; but who they are, and of what kind, they alone manifest to such as are capable of so exalted a knowledge. In fables too, the energies of the gods are imitated; for the world may very properly be called a fable, since bodies, and the corporeal possessions which it contains, are apparent, but souls and intellects are occult and invisible. Besides, to inform all men of the truth concerning the gods, produces contempt in the unwise, from their incapacity of learning, and negligence in the studious; but concealing truth in fables, prevents the contempt of the former, and compels the latter to philosophize. But you will ask why adulteries, thefts, paternal bonds, and other unworthy actions are celebrated in fables? Nor is this unworthy of admiration, that where there is an apparent absurdity, the soul immediately conceiving these discourses to be concealments, may understand that the truth which they contain is to be involved in profound and occult silence[*].

---

[*] In addition to what the philosopher has said in this chapter concerning the utility of fables, we may observe farther, that fables when properly explained, call forth our unperverted conceptions of the gods; give a greater perfection to the divine part of our soul, through that ineffable sympathy which it possesses with more mystic concerns; heal the maladies of our phantasy, purify and illuminate its figured intellections, and elevate it in conjunction with the rational soul to that which is divine.

CHAPTER IV

That there are five Species of Fables; and Examples of each.

OF fables, some are theological, others physical, others animastic, (or belonging to soul,) others material, and lastly, others mixed from these. Fables are theological which employ nothing corporeal, but speculate the very essences of the gods; such as the fable which asserts that Saturn devoured his children: for it obscurely intimates the nature of an intellectual god, since every intellect returns into itself. But we speculate fables physically when we speak concerning the energies of the gods about the World; as when considering Saturn the same as Time, and calling the parts of time the children of the universe, we assert that the children are devoured by their parents. But we employ fables in an animastic mode when we contemplate the energies of soul; because the intellections of our souls, though by a discursive energy they proceed into other things, yet abide in their parents. Lastly, fables are material, such as the Egyptians ignorantly employ, considering and calling corporeal natures divinities; such as Isis, earth; Osiris, humidity; Typhon, heat: or again, denominating Saturn, water; Adonis, fruits; and Bacchus, wine. And, indeed, to assert that these are dedicated to the gods, in the same manner as herbs, stones, and animals, is the part of wise men; but to call them gods is alone the province of mad men; unless we speak in the same manner as when, from established custom, we call the orb of the Sun and its rays the Sun itself. But we may perceive the mixed kind of fables, as well in many other particulars, as in the fable which relates, that Discord at a banquet of the gods threw a golden apple, and that a dispute about it arising among the goddesses, they were sent by Jupiter to take the judgement of Paris, who, charmed with the beauty of Venus, gave her the apple in preference to the rest. For in this fable the banquet denotes the supermundane powers of the gods; and on this account they subsist in conjunction with each other: but the golden apple denotes the world, which, on account of its composition from contrary natures, is not improperly said to be thrown by Discord, or strife. But again, since different gifts are imparted to the world by different gods, they appear to contest with each other for the apple. And a soul living according to sense, (for this is Paris) not perceiving other powers in the universe, asserts that the contended apple subsists alone through the beauty of Venus. But of these species of fables, such as are theological belong to philosophers; the physical and animastic to poets; but the mixed to initiatory rites since the intention of all mystic ceremonies is, to conjoin us with the world and the gods. But if it be requisite to relate another fable, we may employ the following with advantage. It is said that the mother of the gods perceiving Attis by the river Gallus, became in love with him, and having placed on him a starry hat, lived afterwards with him in intimate familiarity; but Attis falling in love with a Nymph, deserted the mother of the gods, and entered into association with the Nymph. Through this the mother of the gods caused Attis to become insane, who cutting off his genital parts, left them with the nymph, and then returned again to his pristine connection with the Goddess. The mother of the gods then is the vivific goddess, and on this account is called mother: but Attis is the Demiurgus of natures conversant with generation and corruption; and hence he is said to be found by the river Gallus; for Gallus denotes the Galaxy, or milky circle, from which a passive body descends to the earth. But since primary gods perfect such as are secondary, the mother of the gods falling in love with Attis imparts to him celestial powers; for this is the meaning of the starry hat. But Attis loves a nymph, and nymphs preside over generation; for every thing in generation flows. But because it is necessary that the flowing nature of generation should be stopped, lest something worse than things last should be produced; in order to accomplish this, the Demiurgus of generable and corruptible natures, sending prolific powers into the realms of generation, is again conjoined with the gods. But these things indeed never took place at any particular time, because they have a perpetuity of subsistence: and intellect contemplates all things as subsisting together; but discourse considers this thing as first, and that as second, in the order of existence. Hence, since a fable most aptly corresponds to the world, how is it possible that we, who are imitators of the world, can be more gracefully ornamented than by the assistance of fable? For through this we observe a festive Day. And, in the first place, we ourselves falling from the celestial regions, and associating with a nymph, the symbol of generation, live immersed in sorrow, abstaining from corn and other gross and sordid aliment; since every thing of this kind is contrary to the soul: afterwards, the incisions of a tree and fasting succeed, as if we would amputate from our nature all farther progress of generation: at length we employ the nutriment of milk, as if passing by this means into a state of regeneration: and lastly, festivity and crowns, and a re-ascent, as it were, to the gods succeed. But the truth of all this is confirmed by the time in which these ceremonies take place; for they are performed about spring and the equinoctial period, when natures in generation cease to be any longer generated, and the days are more extended than the nights, because this period is accommodated to ascending souls. But the rape of Proserpine is fabled to have taken place about the opposite equinoctial; and this rape alludes to the descent of souls. And thus much concerning the mode of considering fables; to our discourse on which subject, may both the gods and the souls of the writers of fables be propitious.

CHAPTER V

Concerning the first Cause.

AFTER this, it is requisite that we should know the first cause, and the orders of gods posterior to the first, together with the nature of the world, of intellect, soul, and essence; likewise that we should speculate providence, fate, and fortune, virtue and vice, and the good and evil forms of republics produced from these; and lastly, that we should consider from whence evil crept into the world. And though each of these requires many and very extended discourses, yet there is no reason why we may not discuss these subjects with brevity, lest mankind should be totally destitute of the knowledge they contain. It is necessary, then, that the first cause should be one; for the monad presides over all multitude, excelling all things in power and goodness, and on this account it is necessary that all things should participate of its nature; for nothing can hinder its energies through power, and it will not separate itself from any thing on account of the goodness which it possesses. But if the first cause were soul, all things would be animated; if intellect, all things would be intellectual; if essence, all things would participate of essence; which last some perceiving to subsist in all things, have taken occasion to denominate him essence. If then things had nothing besides being, and did not also possess goodness, this assertion would be true; but if beings subsist through goodness, and participate of *the good,* it is necessary that the first cause should be super-essential, and *the good:* but the truth of this is most eminently evinced in souls endued with virtue, and through good neglecting the care of their being, when they expose themselves to the most imminent dangers for their country or friends, or in the cause of virtue. But after this ineffable power the orders of the gods succeed.

CHAPTER VI

Concerning the super-mundane and mundane Gods.

BUT of the gods some are mundane and others super-mundane. I call those mundane who fabricate the world: but of the super-mundane, some produce essences, others intellect, and others soul; and on this account they are distinguished into three orders, in discourses concerning which orders, it is easy to discover all the gods. But of the mundane gods, some are the causes of the world's existence, others animate the world; others again harmonize it, thus composed from different natures; and others, lastly, guard and preserve it when harmonically arranged. And since these orders are four, and each consists from things first, middle, and last, it is necessary that the disposers of these should be twelve: hence Jupiter, Neptune, and Vulcan, fabricate the world; Ceres, Juno, and Diana, animate it; Mercury, Venus, and Apollo, harmonize it; and, lastly, Vesta, Minerva, and Mars, preside over it with a guardian power[*]. But the truth of this may be seen in statues as in ænigmas: for Apollo harmonizes the lyre, Pallas is invested with arms, and Venus is naked; since harmony generates beauty, and beauty is not concealed in objects of sensible inspection. But since these gods primarily possess the world, it is necessary to consider the other gods as subsisting in these; as Bacchus in Jupiter, Esculapius in

---

[*] Such of my English readers as are capable of ascending to a knowledge of the gods, through a regular course of philosophic discipline, may consult my translation of the Elements of Theology, by Proclus, my Introduction to the Parmenides of Plato, and my Notes on the Cratylus; where the orders of the gods are more fully unfolded.

Apollo, and the Graces in Venus. We may likewise behold the orbs with which they are connected; *i.e.* Vesta with earth, Neptune with water, Juno with air, and Vulcan with fire. But the six superior gods we denominate from general custom; for we assume Apollo and Diana for the sun and moon; but we attribute the orb of Saturn to Ceres, æther to Pallas; and we assert that heaven is common to them all. The orders, therefore, powers, and spheres of the twelve gods, are thus unfolded by us, and celebrated as in a sacred hymn.

CHAPTER VII

On the Nature and Perpetuity of the World.

It is necessary that the world should be incorruptible and unbegotten: incorruptible, for this being corrupted, it must either produce one better, or one worse, or disordered confusion; but if by corruption it becomes worse, its artificer must be evil, who thus changes it from better to worse; but if it becomes better, its artificer must be defective in power, because he did not fabricate it better at first; but if through corruption he changes it into the same state as before, he labours in vain. And it is not lawful to assert that he changes it into nothing but disorder and confusion: from all which it is sufficiently evident that the world is unbegotten: for if it be incapable of corruption, it is unbegotten; since every thing generated is also corrupted. We may likewise add, that since the world subsists through the goodness of divinity, it is necessary that divinity should always be good, and the world perpetually endure: just in the same manner as light is coexistent with the sun and fire, and the shadow with its forming body. But of the bodies contained in the world, some imitate intellect, and revolve in a circle; but others soul, and are moved in a right line. And of those which are moved in a right line, fire and air, are impelled upwards, but water and earth downwards: but of those which revolve in a circle, the inerratic sphere commences its motion from the east, but the seven planets are carried in their orbits from the west. But of this there are many causes, among which the following is not the least; that if there was but one rapid period of the orbs, generation would be imperfect: but since there is a diversity of motion, it is also requisite that there should be a difference in the nature of bodies. It is, besides this, necessary that a celestial body should neither burn nor produce cold, nor generate any thing else which is the property of the four elements*. But since the world is a sphere, which the zodiac evinces, and in every sphere the inferior part is the middle, for it is every way much distant from the surface; hence heavy bodies are impelled downwards, and are driven to the earth: and all these indeed the gods fabricate, intellect orderly disposes, and soul perpetually moves. And thus much concerning the gods.

---

* For the reason of this, see my Introduction to the Timæus of Plato.

CHAPTER VIII

Concerning Intellect and Soul; and that Soul is immortal.

BUT there is a certain power subordinate to essence, but prior to soul; from essence indeed deriving its being, but perfecting soul, in the same manner as the sun perfects corporeal sight. And of souls some are rational and immortal, but others irrational and mortal; and the first of these are produced from the first, but the second from the second orders of Gods. But, in the first place, let us investigate the definition of soul. Soul then is that by which animated natures differ from such as are inanimate; but they differ through motion, sense, phantasy, and intelligence*. The irrational soul therefore

---

* In order to understand this distinction properly, it is necessary to observe, that the gnostic powers of the soul are five in number, viz. *intellect, cogitation, opinion, phantasy, sense. Intellect* is that power by which we understand simple self-evident truths, called axioms, and are able to pass into contact with ideas themselves. But *cogitation* is that power which forms and perfects arguments and reasons. *Opinion* is that which knows the universal insensible particulars, as that every man is a biped; and the conclusion of cogitation, as that every rational soul is immortal; but it only knows *that* a thing is, but is perfectly ignorant of the *why* it is. And the *phantasy* is that power which apprehends things cloathed with figure, and may be called *a figured intelligence.* And, lastly, *sense* is that power which is distributed about the organs of sensation; which is mingled with passion in its judgement of things, and apprehends that only which falls upon, and agitates it externally. Again, the basis of the rational life is *opinion*; for the true man, or the rational soul, consists of *intellect, cogitation,* and *opinion*; but the summit of the irrational life is *the phantasy.* And *opinion* and *phantasy* are connected with each other; and the irrational is filled with powers from the rational life: so that the fictitious man commences from the phantasy; under which desire, like a many-headed savage beast, and anger, like a raging

is sensitive and phantastic life; but the rational soul is that which rules over sense and phantasy, and uses reason in its energies. And the irrational soul indeed is subservient to the corporeal passions; for it desires without reason, and is inflamed with anger: but the rational soul through the assistance of reason despises the body, and contending with the irrational soul, when it conquers, produces virtue, but when it is conquered, vice. But it is necessary that the rational soul should be immortal, because it knows the gods; for no thing mortal knows that which is immortal. Besides this, it despises human concerns, as foreign from its nature, and has a disposition contrary to bodies, as being itself incorporeal. Add too, that when the body with which a soul is connected is beautiful and young, then that soul is oppressed and its vigour diminished; but when this grows old, the soul revives, and increases in strength and vigour. And every worthy soul uses intellect; but intellect is not generated by body; for how can things destitute of intellect generate intellect? But employing

---

lion, subsist.

But of these powers, *intellect* and *sense* do not employ a reasoning energy, on account of the acuteness and suddenness of their perceptions. And with respect to *cogitation*, it either assumes the principles of reasoning from intellect, which principles we call axioms; and in this case it produces demonstrative reasoning, the conclusions of which are always true, on account of the certainty of the axioms from which reason receives its increase: or the same *cogitation* converts itself to *opinion*, and deriving its principles from thence, forms dialectic reason, so called from its being employed by men in common discourse with each other; and hence its conclusions are not always true, because *opinion* is sometimes false: or, in the third place, *cogitation* conjoins itself with *the phantasy*, and in consequence of this produces vicious reasoning, which always embraces that which false.

the body as an instrument, it does not subsist in body: in the same manner as no artificer of machines subsists in his machines; and yet many of these, without any one touching them, are moved from place to place. But we ought not to wonder if the rational soul is often led astray by the body; for arts themselves when their instruments are damaged are incapable of operation.

CHAPTER IX

Concerning Providence, Fate, and Fortune.

FROM hence also we may perceive the providence of the gods; for how could order be inserted in the world if there be no one who distributes it in order? From whence too could all things be produced for the sake of something; as, for instance, the irrational soul that there might be sense; the rational, that the earth might be adorned? From natural effects likewise we may perceive the operations of providence[*]: for it has constructed the eyes of a diaphanous nature for the purpose of seeing; but the nostrils above the mouth, that we might distinguish disagreeable smells: and of the teeth, the middle are fashioned sharp, for the purpose of cutting, but those situated in the more interior part of the mouth are broad, for the purpose of bruising the aliment in pieces. And thus we may perceive in all things, that nothing is constructed without reason and design. But since so much providence is displayed in the last of things, it is impossible that it should not subsist in such as are first: besides, divinations, and the healing of bodies, take place from the beneficent providence of the gods. And it is necessary to believe that a similar concern about the world is exerted by the gods, without either expecting reward, or enduring labour in the exertion; but that as bodies endued with power, produce essentially, or by their very essence, that which they produce; as the sun illuminates and heats by that which he is alone; so the providence of the gods, by a much greater reason, without labour and difficulty to itself,

---

[*] See more on this interesting subject in my translation of Plotinus on Providence.

confers good on the subjects of its providential exertions. So that by this means the objections of the Epicureans against providence are dissolved: for, say they, that which is divine is neither the cause of molestation to itself nor to others. And such is the incorporeal providence of the gods about bodies and souls. But the beneficent exertion of the gods resulting from, and subsisting in, bodies, is different from the former, and is called fate, because its series is more apparent in bodies; and for the sake of which also the mathematical art was invented. That human affairs therefore, and particularly a corporeal nature, are not only directed by the gods, but from divine bodies also, is highly consonant to reason and truth; and hence reason dictates, that health and sickness, prosperous and adverse fortune, proceed from these according to every one's particular deserts. But to refer injustice and crimes committed through lasciviousness and wantonness to fate, leaves us indeed good, but the gods evil and base: unless some one should endeavour to remove this consequence, by replying, that every thing which the world contains, and whatever has a natural subsistence, is good, but that the nature which is badly nourished, or which is of a more imbecile condition, changes the good proceeding from fate into something worse; just as the sun, though it is good itself, becomes noxious to the blear-eyed and feverish. For on what account do the Massagetæ devour their parents, the Hebrews use circumcision, and the Persians preserve their nobility? But how can astrologers call Saturn and Mars noxious, and yet again celebrate these planets as beneficent, by asserting that philosophy, kingdoms, and military command, are their gifts? If they assign triangles and squares as the cause, it is absurd that human virtue should every where remain the same, but that the gods should be subject to mutation from diversity of places. But that nobility or ignobility of parents may be predicted from the stars, shews that they do not produce all things, but only signify some, by their different situations and aspects; for how can things which subsisted prior to generation be produced from generation? As therefore providence and fate subsist about nations and cities, as likewise about every individual of human kind, so also fortune, about which it is now requisite to speak. Fortune, therefore, must be considered as a power of the gods, disposing things differing from each other, and happening contrary to expectation, to beneficent purposes[*]; and on this account it is proper that cities should celebrate this goddess in common; since every city is composed from different particulars. But this goddess holds her dominion in sublunary concerns, since every thing fortuitous is excluded from the regions above the moon. But if the evil enjoy prosperous fortune, and the worthy are oppressed with want, there is nothing wonderful in such a dispensation; for the former consider riches as all things, but they are despised by the latter. And besides this, prosperous events do not diminish the depravity of the evil; but virtue is alone sufficient to the good.

---

[*] Fortune may likewise be defined, that deific distribution which causes every thing to fill up the lot assigned to it, by the condition of its being; and as that divine power which congregates all sublunary causes, and enables them to confer on sublunary effects that particular good which their nature and merits eminently deserve.

CHAPTER X

Concerning Virtue and Vice.

BUT in discoursing on the soul it is requisite to speak of virtue and vice; for while the irrational soul proceeding into bodies immediately produces anger and desire, the rational soul presiding over these, causes the whole soul to receive a tripartite division, viz. into reason, anger, and desire. But the virtue of reason is prudence, of anger, fortitude; of desire, temperance; and of the whole soul, justice. For it is requisite that reason should judge what is fit and becoming; that anger, listening to the persuasions of reason, should despise things apparently horrible; and that desire should pursue that which is attended with reason, and not that which is apparently pleasant. And when the parts of the soul are in this condition, a just life is the result: for justice respecting possessions is but a small part of virtue. Hence in well-educated men you will perceive all these in amicable conjunction; but in the uncultivated, one is bold and unjust; another temperate and foolish; and another prudent and in temperate: all which you cannot call virtues, because they are destitute of reason, imperfect, and belong to certain irrational animals. But vice is to be considered from contraries; for the vice of reason is folly; of anger, fear; of desire, intemperance; and of the whole soul, injustice. But virtues are produced from an upright polity, and from a well-ordered education and instruction; but vices from an opposite process.

CHAPTER XI

Concerning a good and depraved Polity.

But the forms of polities are produced according to the triple division of the soul; for the rulers are assimilated to reason, the soldiers to anger, and the common people to desire. Hence, when all things are administered according to reason, and he who is the best of all men possesses dominion, then a kingdom is produced: but when, from reason and anger in conjunction, more than one hold the reins of government, an aristocracy is produced: but where government is carried on through desire, and honours subsist with a view to possessions, such a polity is called a timocracy; and that polity which takes place in opposition to a kingdom is called a tyranny; for the former administers every thing, but the latter nothing, according to reason. But an oligarchy, or the dominion of a few, is contrary to an aristocracy; because in the former, not the best, but a few only, and those the worst, govern the city. And lastly, a democracy is opposed to a timocracy; because in the former, not such as abound in riches, but the multitude alone, is the ruler of all things[*].

---

[*] All the forms of polities mentioned in this chapter are accurately discussed in Plato's Republic, which the reader will do well to study, together with the fragments of the Commentaries of Proclus. on that inimitable work.

CHAPTER XII

*From whence Evils originate, and that
there is not a nature of Evil.*

BUT how came evil into the world, since the gods are good, and the producing causes of all things? And, in the first place, we ought to assert that since the gods are good, and the authors of all things, there is not any nature of evil, but that it is produced by the absence of good; just as darkness is of itself nothing, but is produced by the privation of light. But if evil has any subsistence, it must necessarily subsist either in the gods or in intellects, in souls or in bodies: but it cannot subsist in the gods, since every god is good. And if any one should say that intellect is evil, he must at the same time assert that intellect is deprived of intellect: but if soul, he must affirm that soul is worse than body; for every body, considered according to itself, is without evil. But if they assert that evil subsists from soul and body conjoined, it will certainly be absurd, that things which separately considered are not evil, should become evil from their conjunction with each other. But if any one should say that dæmons are evil, we reply, that if they possess their power from the gods they will not be evil; but if from something else, then the gods will not be the authors of all things: and if the gods do not produce all things, either they are willing but not able, or they are able but not willing; but neither of these can be ascribed with any propriety to a god. And from hence it is manifest that there is nothing in the world naturally evil; but about the energies of men, and of these not all, nor yet always, evil appears. Indeed, if men were guilty through evil itself, nature herself would be evil; but if he who commits adultery considers the adultery as evil, but the pleasure connected with it as good; if he who is guilty of homicide considers the slaughter as evil, but the riches resulting from the deed as good; and if he who brings destruction on his enemies considers the destruction as evil, but taking revenge on an enemy as good; and souls are by this means guilty; hence evils will be produced through goodness, just as while light is absent darkness is produced, which at the same time has no subsistence in the nature of things. The soul therefore becomes guilty because it desires good, but it wanders about good because it is not the first essence. But that it may not wander, and that when it does so, proper remedies may be applied, and it may be restored, many things have been produced by the gods; for arts and sciences, virtues and prayers, sacrifices and initiations, laws and polities, judgements and punishments, were invented for the purpose of preventing souls from falling into guilt; and even when they depart from the present body, expiatory gods and dæmons purify them from guilt.

CHAPTER XIII

After what Manner Things perpetual are said to be generated.*

CONCERNING the gods therefore, the world, and human affairs, what has been said may be sufficient for such as are not able to be led upwards through the assistance of philosophy, and yet do not possess incurable souls. It now remains that we speak concerning natures which were never generated nor separated from one another; since we have already observed, that secondary are produced from primary natures. Every thing which is generated is either generated by art, or by nature, or according to power. It is necessary therefore that every thing operating according to nature or art should be prior to the things produced; but that things operating according to power, should have their productions co-existent with themselves; since they likewise possess an inseparable power: just as the sun produces light co-existent with itself; fire, heat; and snow, coldness. If therefore the gods produced the world by art, they would not cause it simply to be, but to be in some

---

* The Platonic philosophy makes a just and beautiful distinction between *the perpetual*, and *the eternal*. "For *the eternal*," says Olympiodorus, "is a total now exempt from the past and future circulations of time, and totally subsisting in a present abiding now: but *the perpetual* subsists indeed always, but is beheld in the three parts of time, the past, present, and future: hence we call God *eternal* on account of his being unconnected with time; but we do not denominate him *perpetual*, because he does not subsist in time." Olympiodorus in Arist. Meteor. p. 32. Hence the world may be properly called *perpetual*, but not *eternal*, as Boethius well ob serves; and the philosopher Sallust well knowing this distinction, uses, with great accuracy, the word *perpetual* in this chapter instead of the word *eternal*.

particular manner; for all art produces form. From whence therefore does the world derive its being? If from nature, since nature in fabricating imparts something of itself to its productions and the gods are incorporeal, it is necessary that the world (the offspring of the gods) should be incorporeal. But if any one says that the gods are corporeal, from whence does the power of incorporeals originate? And besides, if this be admitted, the world being corrupted, its artificer also must necessarily be corrupted, on the hypothesis that he operates according to nature. It remains therefore that the gods produced the world by power alone; but every thing generated by power, subsists together with the cause containing this power: and hence productions of this kind cannot be destroyed unless the producing cause is deprived of power. So that those who subject the world to corruption*, plainly deny that there are gods; or if they assert that there are gods, they deprive divinity of power. He therefore who produced all things through power, caused all things to be co-existent with himself. And since this power is the greatest possible, not only men and animals were produced, but also gods and dæmons. And as much as the first god differs from our nature, by so much is it necessary that there should be more powers situated between us and him†; for all natures which are much distant from each other possess a multitude of connecting mediums.

---

* Meaning the Christians.
† For a more ample confirmation of the necessity that there should be gods posterior to the first, see p. 263 of my Introduction to the Parmenides.

CHAPTER XIV

*How the Gods who are immutable are
said to be angry and appeased.*

BUT if any one thinking agreeable to reason and truth, that the gods are immutable, doubts how they rejoice in the good, but are averse from the evil; and how they become angry with the guilty, but are rendered propitious by proper cultivation; we reply, that divinity neither rejoices; for that which rejoices is also influenced by sorrow: nor is angry; for anger is a passion: nor is appeased with gifts; for then he would be influenced by delight. Nor is it lawful that a divine nature should be well or ill affected from human concerns; for the divinities are perpetually good and profitable, but are never noxious, and ever subsist in the same uniform mode of being. But we, when we are good, are conjoined with the gods through similitude; but when evil, We are separated from them through dissimilitude. And while we live ac cording to virtue, we partake of the gods, but when we become evil we cause them to become our enemies; not that they are angry, but because guilt prevents us from receiving the illuminations of the gods, and subjects us to the power of avenging dæmons. But if we obtain pardon of our guilt through prayers and sacrifices, we neither appease nor cause any mutation to take place in the gods; but by methods of this kind, and by our conversion to a divine nature, we apply a remedy to our vices, and again become partakers of the goodness of the gods. So that it is the same thing to assert that divinity is turned from the evil, as to say that the sun is concealed from those who are deprived of sight.

CHAPTER XV

Why we honour the Gods, who are not indigent of any Thing.

FROM hence we are presented with a solution of the doubts concerning sacrifices and other particulars relative to the cultivation of divinity; for that which is divine is not indigent of any thing. But the honours which we pay to the gods, are performed for the sake of our advantage: and since the providence of the gods is every where extended, a certain habitude, or fitness, is all that is requisite in order to receive their beneficent communications. But all habitude is produced through imitation and similitude; and hence temples imitate the heavens, but altars the earth; statues resemble life, and on this account they are similar to animals; and prayers imitate that which is intellectual; but characters, superior ineffable powers; herbs and stones resemble matter; and animals which are sacrificed, the irrational life of our souls. But from all these no thing happens to the gods beyond what they already possess; for what accession can be made to a divine nature? But a conjunction with our souls and the gods is by this means produced.

CHAPTER XVI

Concerning Sacrifices and other Honours which are of no Advantage to the Gods, but are useful to Men.

BUT I think it will be proper to add a few things concerning sacrifices. And, in the first place, since we possess every thing from the gods, and it is but just to offer the first fruits of gifts to the givers; hence, of our possessions we offer the first fruits through consecrated gifts; of our bodies, through ornaments; and of our life, through sacrifices. Besides, without sacrifices prayers are words only; but accompanied with sacrifices they become animated words; the words indeed corroborating life, but life animating the words. Add too that the felicity of every thing is its proper perfection; but the proper perfection of every thing consists in a conjunction with its cause: and on this account we pray that we may be conjoined with the gods. Since therefore life primarily subsists in the gods, and there is also a certain human life, but the latter desires to be united with the former, a medium is required; for natures much distant from each other cannot be conjoined without a medium; and it is necessary that the medium should be similar to the connected natures. Life therefore must necessarily be the medium of life; and hence men of the present day, that are happy, and all the ancients, have sacrificed animals; and this indeed not rashly, but in a manner accommodated to every god, with many other ceremonies respecting the cultivation of divinity. And thus much concerning sacrifices and the worship of the gods.

CHAPTER XVII

That the World is naturally incorruptible.

THAT the gods will never destroy the world has been already asserted; but the order of discourse requires that we should now prove that it is naturally incorruptible; for whatever is corrupted is either corrupted from itself or from some other nature. If therefore the world is corrupted from itself, fire must necessarily burn itself, and water consume itself by dryness: but if the world may be corrupted by another, it must either be from body or from that which is incorporeal. But it is impossible that this can be effected from that which is incorporeal; for incorporeals, such as nature and soul, preserve corporeal substances; and nothing is destroyed by that which naturally preserves. But if the world may be corrupted by body, it must either be from the bodies which exist at present, or from others. And if from the bodies existing at present, either those which move in a circle must destroy those moving in a right line, or those moving in a right line, such as circularly revolve. But nothing moving in a circle has a corruptible nature; for why do we never see any thing of this kind corrupted? And things proceeding in a right line cannot reach those revolving in an orb; for if this were possible, why have they never been able to accomplish this to the present day? But neither can the natures which are moved in a right line be destroyed by each other; for the corruption of one is the generation of the other; and this is not destruction, but mutation alone. But if the world may be corrupted by other bodies than those which it contains, it is impossible to tell from whence these bodies were generated, or in what place they at present exist.

Besides, whatever is corrupted, is either corrupted in form or matter; but form is figure, and matter is body. And when forms are corrupted, but the matter remains, then we perceive that something else is generated: but if matter may be corrupted, how comes it to pass that it has not failed in so great a number of years? But if instead of the corrupted natures others are produced, they are either generated from beings or from non-beings; and if from beings, since these remain perpetually, matter also must be eternal: but if beings (or the things which are) suffer corruption, the authors of this hypothesis must assert, that not only the world, but all things, will be corrupted. But if matter is generated from non-beings, in the first place, it is impossible that any thing can be generated from non-beings: and even if this were possible, and matter could be thus produced, as long as non-being subsists matter would continue in existence; and non-beings can never be destroyed. And if they say that matter is without form, in the first place, why does this happen not according to a part, but to the whole world? And in the next place, bodies themselves would not be destroyed, but only their beauty. Besides, whatever is corrupted is either dissolved into the natures from which it consists, or vanishes into nonentity; but if it be dissolved into the natures from which it is composed, others again will be produced: for on what account was it produced at first? But if beings pass into that which is not, what should hinder this from happening to divinity itself? If power prevents, it is not the property of power to preserve itself alone: and, by a similar reason, it is impossible that beings should be generated from non-beings, and that they should vanish into non-entity. Likewise it is necessary that the world, if it may be corrupted, should either be corrupted according or contrary to nature. But if it may be corrupted according to nature, then, on account of its past and present continuance in being, it would possess that which is contrary, prior to that which is agreeable, to nature; but if contrary to nature, then it is requisite that there should be some other nature which may change the nature of the world; and which is nowhere apparent. Besides, whatever is capable of being naturally corrupted, we also are able to destroy; but no one has ever destroyed or changed the circular body of the world; while, on the other hand, we can change, but cannot destroy, an elementary body. And, lastly, whatever may be corrupted is changed and grows old by time; but through such an extended succession of ages, the world has remained without mutation. And having said thus much to those who require on this subject stronger demonstrations, we earnestly supplicate the world to be propitious to our undertaking.

CHAPTER XVIII

*Why Sacrifices are performed,
and that Divinity cannot be injured.*

BUT impiety, which invades some places of the earth*, and which will often subsist in future, ought not to give any disturbance to the worthy mind; for things of this kind do not affect, nor can religious honours be of any advantage to the gods; and the soul, from its middle nature, is not always able to pursue that which is right. Nor can the whole world participate in a similar manner of the providence of the gods; but some of its parts enjoy this eternally and others according to time; some possess this primarily and others in a secondary degree: just as the head perceives from all the senses, but the whole body from one alone. And on this account, as it appears to me, those who instituted festive days, appointed also such as are inauspicious; during which some particulars belonging to sacred rites are omitted, and others are shut up; but such things as expiate the imbecility of our nature deprive certain particulars of their peculiar ornament. Besides it is not improbable that impiety is a species of punishment; for those who have known, and at the same time despised the gods, we may reasonably suppose will, in another life, be deprived of the knowledge of their nature. And those who have honoured their proper sovereigns as gods, shall be cut off from the divinities, as the punishment of their impiety.

---

* The philosopher alludes here to the Christian religion.

CHAPTER XIX

Why Offenders are not immediately punished.

NOR ought we to wonder if not only offenders of this kind, but likewise others, are not immediately punished for their guilt; for there are not only dæmons who punish offending souls, but souls also inflict punishment on themselves; and it is not proper that such as are calculated, through the enormity of their guilt, to suffer for the whole of time, should be punished in a small part of time. Besides it is requisite that there should be such a thing as human virtue: but if the guilty were immediately punished, men, from being just through fear, would no longer be virtuous. But souls are punished on their departure from the present body; some by wandering about this part of the earth, others in certain of its hot or cold regions, and others are tormented by avenging dæmons. But universally the rational soul suffers punishment in conjunction with the irrational soul, the partner of its guilt; and through this that shadowy body* derives its subsistence, which is beheld about sepulchres, and especially about the tombs of such as have lived an abandoned life.

---

* See my Introduction to, and translation of, Plato's Phædo.

CHAPTER XX

Concerning the Transmigration of Souls; and how rational are said to be carried in irrational Natures.

BUT the transmigrations of souls, if they take place into such as are rational, then they become the souls of particular bodies; if into such as are irrational, they follow externally, in the same manner as our presiding dæmons attend us in their beneficent operations[*]; for the rational part never becomes the soul of the irrational nature. But the truth of transmigration is evinced by the circumstances which take place from the birth of individuals; for why are some born blind, others imbecil, and others with a vicious soul? And besides, since souls are naturally adapted to perform their peculiar employments in bodies, it is not proper that when they have once deserted them they should remain indolent for ever; for if souls did not return again into bodies, it is necessary that either they should be infinite in number, or that others should be continually produced by the divinity. But there can be nothing actually infinite in the world; for that which is infinite can never exist in that which is finite. But neither is it possible that others can be produced; for every thing in which something new may be generated is necessarily imperfect; but it is requisite that the world should be perfect, because it is produced from a perfect nature.

---

[*] This beautiful doctrine, which seems to have originated from Syrianus and Proclus, was universally adopted by all the succeeding Platonists.

CHAPTER XXI

That both in this Life, and when they depart from it, the good will be happy.

BUT souls that live according to virtue shall, in other respects, be happy; and when separated from the irrational nature, and purified from all body, shall be conjoined with the gods, and govern the whole world, together with the deities by whom it was produced. And, indeed, though nothing of this kind should happen to the soul, yet virtue herself, and the pleasure and glory resulting from virtue, together with a life free from sorrow, and subjection to others, would be sufficient to produce felicity in those who choose, and are able to pursue, a life wholly conformable to virtue itself.

THE
PYTHAGORIC SENTENCES
OF
DEMOPHILUS

THE
PYTHAGORIC SENTENCES
OF
DEMOPHILUS

REQUEST not of the divinity such things as when obtained you cannot preserve; for no gift of divinity can ever be taken away; and on this account he does not confer that which you are unable to retain.

Be vigilant in your intellectual part; for sleep about this has an affinity with real death.

Divinity sends evil to men, not as being influenced by anger, but for the sake of purification; for anger is foreign from divinity, since it arises from circumstances taking place contrary to the will: but no thing contrary to the will can happen to a god.

When you deliberate whether or not you shall injure another, you will previously suffer the evil yourself which you intended to commit: but neither must you expect any good from the evil; for the manners of every one are correspondent to his life and actions: for every soul is a repository; that which is good, of things good, and that which is evil, of things depraved.

After long consultation, engage either in speaking or acting; for you have not the ability to recall either your discourses or deeds.

Divinity does not principally esteem the tongue, but the deeds of the wise; for a wise man, even when he is silent, honours divinity.

A loquacious and ignorant man, both in prayer and sacrifice, contaminates a divine nature: the wise man therefore is alone a priest, is alone the friend of divinity, and only knows how to pray.

The wise man being sent hither naked, should naked invoke him by whom he was sent; for he alone is heard by divinity who is not burthened with foreign concerns.

It is impossible to receive from divinity any gift greater than virtue[*].

Gifts and victims confer no honour on the divinity, nor is he adorned with offerings suspended in temples; but a soul divinely inspired, solidly conjoins us with divinity; for it is necessary that like should approach to like.

It is more painful to be subservient to passions than to tyrants themselves.

It is better to converse more with yourself than with others.

If you are always careful to remember, that in whatever place either your soul or body accomplishes

---

[*] Because virtue is the perfection of life, and the proper perfection of any being is the felicity of that being.

any deed, divinity is present as an inspector of your conduct; in all your discourses and actions you will venerate the presence of an inspector from whom nothing can be concealed, and will at the same time possess divinity as an intimate associate.

Believe that you are furious and insane, in proportion as you are ignorant of yourself.

It is necessary to search for those wives and children which will remain after a liberation from the present life.

The self-sufficient and needy philosopher lives a life truly similar to divinity, and considers the non-possession of external and unnecessary goods as the greatest wealth; for the acquisition of riches sometimes in flames desire; but not to act in any respect unjustly is sufficient to the enjoyment of a blessed life.

True goods are never produced by indolent habits.

Esteem that to be eminently good, which, when communicated to another, will be increased to yourself[*].

Esteem those to be eminently your friends, who assist your soul rather than your body.

Consider both the praise and reproach of every foolish person as ridiculous, and the whole life of an ignorant man as a disgrace.

Endeavour that your familiars may reverence rather

---

[*] And this is the case with intellectual goods.

than fear you; for love attends upon reverence, but hatred upon fear.

The sacrifices of fools are the aliment of the fire; but the offerings which they suspend in temples are the supplies of the sacrilege.

Understand that no dissimulation can be long concealed.

The unjust man suffers greater evil while his soul is tormented with a consciousness of guilt, than when his body is scourged with whips.

It is by no means safe to discourse concerning divinity with men of false opinions; for the danger is equally great in speaking to such as these things either fallacious or true.

By everywhere using reason as your guide, you will avoid the commission of crimes.

By being troublesome to others, you will not easily escape molestation yourself.

Consider that as great erudition, through which you are able to bear the want of erudition in the ignorant.

He who is depraved does not listen to the divine law; and on this account lives without law.

A just man, who is a stranger, is not only superior to a citizen, but is even more excellent than a relation.

As many passions of the soul, so many fierce and savage despots.

No one is free who has not obtained the empire of himself.

Labour, together with continence, precedes the acquisition of every good.

Be persuaded that those things are not your riches which you do not possess in the penetralia of cogitation.

Do that which you judge to be beautiful and honest, though you should acquire no glory from the performance; for the vulgar is a depraved judge of beautiful deeds.

Make trial of a man rather from his deeds than his discourses; for many live badly and speak well.

Perform great things, at the same time promising nothing great.

Since the roots of our natures are established in divinity, from which also we are produced, we should tenaciously adhere to our root; for streams also of water, and other offspring of the earth, when their roots are cut off become rotten and dry.

The strength of the soul is temperance; for this is the light of a soul destitute of passions: but it is much better to die than to darken the soul through the intemperance of the body.

You cannot easily denominate that man happy who depends either on his friends or children, or on any fleeting and fallen nature; for all these are unstable and uncertain; but to depend on one's self and on divinity is alone stable and firm.

He is a wise man, and beloved by divinity, who studies how to labour for the good of his soul, as much as others labour for the sake of the body.

Yield all things to their kindred and ruling nature except liberty.

Learn how to produce eternal children, not such as may supply the wants of the body in old age, but such as may nourish the soul with perpetual food.

It is impossible that the same person can be *a lover of pleasure*, *a lover of body*, *a lover of riches*, and *a lover of divinity*: for a lover of pleasure is also a lover of body; but a lover of body is entirely a lover of riches; but a lover of riches is necessarily unjust; and the unjust is necessarily profane towards divinity, and lawless with respect to men. Hence, though he should sacrifice hecatombs, he is only by this means the more impious, unholy, atheistical, and sacrilegious with respect to his intention: and on this account it is necessary to avoid every lover of pleasure as an atheist and polluted person.

The divinity has not a place in the earth more allied to his nature than a pure and holy soul.

THE
HYMNS
OF
PROCLUS

To the Sun

Hear golden Titan! king of mental fire,
Ruler of light; to thee supreme belongs
The splendid key of life's prolific fount;
And from on high thou pour'st harmonic streams
In rich abundance into matter's worlds.*
Hear! for high rais'd above th' ætherial plains,
And in the world's bright middle orb† thou reign'st,
Whilst all things by thy sov'reign power are fill'd
With mind-exciting, providential care.
The starry fires surround thy vigorous fire, to
And ever in unweary'd, ceaseless dance,
O'er earth wide-bosom'd, vivid dew diffuse.
By thy perpetual and repeated course
The hours and seasons in succession rise;
And hostile elements their conflicts cease,
Soon as they view thy awful beams, great king,
From deity ineffable and secret born.‡

---

* *Matter's worlds.* According to the Chaldaic theology, there are seven corporeal worlds, viz. one empyrean, three ætherial, and three material, which last three consist of the inerratic sphere, the seven planetary spheres, and the sublunary region. But the empyrean and ætherial worlds, when compared with the three last, are said to be immaterial, not that they are void of matter, but because the matter from which they are composed bears the relation of an immaterial essence to that of the other worlds, from the extreme purity and vitality of its nature. I only add, that according to the same theology, the sun moves beyond the inerratic sphere in the last of the etherial worlds. See more concerning this in my notes to the Cratylus.
† That is, in the last ætherial world, which is of course the middle of the seven worlds.
‡ That is, from the first cause, or the good. But the sun is said, by way of eminence, to be the progeny of this highest god, on

The steady Parcæ, at thy high command,
The fatal thread of mortal life roll back;
For wide-extended, sov'reign sway is thine.
From thy fair series of attractive song,
Divinely charming, Phoebus into light
Leaps forth exulting; and with god-like harp,
To rapture strung, the raging uproar lulls
Of dire-resounding Hyle's mighty flood.*
From thy bland dance, repelling deadly ill,
Salubrious Pæan blossoms into light,
Health far diffusing, and th' extended world
With streams of harmony innoxious fills.
Thee too they celebrate in sacred hymns
Th' illustrious source whence mighty Bacchus came;
And thee in matter's utmost stormy depths
Euion† Ate they for ever sing.
But others found thy praise in tuneful verse,
As fam'd Adonis, delicate and fair.
Ferocious dæmons, noxious to mankind,‡

---

    account of the analogy which he bears to him in his illuminations. For as the good is the source of the light of the intelligible world, so Apollo gives light to the supermundane, and the sun to the sensible, worlds.

*   I have used the word *Hyle*, or *matter*, instead of *generation*, which is employed by Proclus, because it is better adapted to the measure of the verses; but the meaning of each word is nearly the same, for the regions of matter are the regions of generation.

†   An epithet of Bacchus.

‡   According to the most accurate division of the Demoniacal order, there are six species of dæmons, as we learn from the excellent Olympiodorus, in his Commentary on the Phædo of Plato. The first of these species is called *divine*, from subsisting according to *the one*, or that which is superessential in the mundane gods; the second is denominated *intellectual*, from subsisting according to the intellect of these gods; the third is *rational*, from subsisting according to the soul with which the mundane gods are connected; the fourth is *natural*, being characterized from the

Dread the dire anger of thy rapid scourge;
Dæmons, who machinate a thousand ills,
Pregnant with ruin to our wretched souls,
That merg'd beneath life's dreadful-sounding sea,
In body's chains severely they may toil,
Nor e'er remember in the dark abyss
The splendid palace of their sire sublime.
O best of gods, blest dæmon crown'd with fire,
Image of nature's all-producing god,[*]
And the soul's leader to the realms of light—
Hear! and refine me from the stains of guilt;

> nature which depends on these gods; the fifth is *corporeal*, subsisting according to their bodies; and the sixth is *material*, subsisting according to the matter which depends on these divinities. Or we may say, that some of these dæmons are *celestial*, others *etherial*, and others *aerial*; that some are *aquatic*, others *terrestrial*, and others *subterranean*. Olympiodorus adds, that irrational dæmons commence from the aerial species; in proof of which he cites the following verse from some oracles, (most probably from the Zoroastrian oracles:)
>
> "Being the charioteer of the aerial, terrestrial, and aquatic dogs."

For evil dæmons, as I have shewn in my Dissertation on the Mysteries, appear in the shape of dogs. And perhaps in this verse the sun is the charioteer alluded to, as it wonderfully agrees with what Proclus says of that deity in the verses before us. I only add, that when irrational dæmons are said to be evil, this must not be understood as if they were essentially evil, but that they are noxious only from their employment; that is, from their either calling forth the vices of depraved souls that they may be punished and cured, or from their inflicting punishment alone: for, indeed, there is not anything essentially evil in the universe; for as the cause of all is goodness itself, everything subsisting from thence must be endued with the form of good; since it is not the property of fire to refrigerate, nor of light to give obscurity, nor of goodness to produce from itself anything evil.

[*] That is, image of the first cause.

The supplication of my tears receive,
And heal my wounds defil'd with noxious gore;
The punishments incurr'd by sin remit,
And mitigate the swift, sagacious eye
Of sacred justice, boundless in its view.
By thy pure law, dread evil's constant foe,
Direct my steps, and pour thy sacred light
In rich abundance on my clouded soul:
Dispel the dismal and malignant shades
Of darkness, pregnant with invenom'd ills,
And to my body proper strength afford,
With health, whose presence splendid gifts imparts.
Give lasting fame; and may the sacred care
With which the fair-hair'd muses gifts, of old
My pious ancestors preserv'd, be mine.
Add, if it please thee, all-bestowing god,
Enduring riches, piety's reward;
For power omnipotent invests thy throne,
With strength immense and universal rule.
And if the whirling spindle of the fates
Threats from the starry webs pernicion dire,
Thy sounding shafts with force resistless fend,
And vanquish ere it fall th' impending ill.

To the MUSES*

A SACRED light I sing, which leads on high
Jove's nine fam'd daughters, ruler of the sky,
Whose splendours beaming o'er this sea of life,
On souls hard struggling with its storms of strife,
Through mystic rites perfective and refind,
(From books which stimulate the sluggish mind)
From earth's dire evils leads them to that more,
Where grief and labour can infest no more;
And well instructs them how, with ardent wing,

---

* Proclus, in his Scholia on the Cratylus, beautifully observes as follows, concerning the Muses: "The whole world is bound in indissoluble bonds from Apollo and the Muses, and is both one and all-perfect, through the communications of these divinities; possessing the former through the Apolloniacal monad (Apollo is the monad of the Muses, *i.e.* is the proximately exempt producing cause of their multitude, and in which their summits are fixed like the roots of trees in the earth), but its all-perfect subsistence through the number of the Muses. For the number nine, which is generated from the first perfect number, (that is, three) is, through similitude and sameness, accommodated to the multiform causes of the mundane order and harmony; all of them at the same time being collected into one summit for the purpose of producing one consummate perfection; for the Muses generate the variety of reasons with which the world is replete; but Apollo comprehends in union all the multitude of these. And the Muses give subsistence to the harmony of soul; but Apollo is the leader of intellectual and indivisible harmony. The Muses distribute the phenomena according to harmonical reasons; but Apollo comprehends unapparent and separate harmony. And though both give subsistence to the same things, yet the Muses effect this according to number, but Apollo according to union. And the Muses indeed distribute the unity of Apollo; but Apollo unites and contains harmonic multitude: for the multitude of the Muses proceeds from the essence of *Musagetes*, which is both separate and subsists according to the nature of *the one*."

From Lethe's deep, wide-spreading flood to spring,
And how once more their kindred stars to gain,
And antient feats in truth's immortal plain,
From whence they wand'ring fell, thro' mad desire
Of matter's regions and allotments dire.
In me this rage repress, illustrious Nine!
And fill my mental eye with light divine.
Oh may the doctrines of the wise inspire
My soul with sacred Bacchanalian fire,
Lest men, with filthy piety replete,[*]
From paths of beauteous light divert my feet.
Conduct my erring soul to sacred light,
From wand'ring generation's stormy night:
Wife thro' your volumes hence, the task be mine,
To sing in praise of eloquence divine,
Whose soothing power can charm the troubled soul,
And throbbing anguish and despair controul.
Hear, splendid goddesses, of bounteous mind,
To whom the helm of wisdom is assign'd,
And who the soul with all-attractive flame
Lead to the blest immortals whence she came,
From night profound enabling her to rise,
Forsake dull earth, and gain her native skies,
And with unclouded splendour fill the mind,
By rites ineffable of hymns refin'd.

---

[*] Proclus here, I have no doubt, alludes to the Christians, and particularly to the Catholics, who were not in his days (the fifth century) a sect as they now are. But the reason why he calls them men full of *filthy piety* is, we may presume, in the first place, because they worshipped a *mere man* as the first cause, which is certainly not only a *filthy*, but a *horrid* species of impiety; and in the next place, because they prayed to the departed souls of men who, when living, professed this *filthy piety*, which was still rendering their impiety more odious and impure.

Hear, mighty saviours! and with holy light,
While reading works divine illume my sight,
And dissipate these mists, that I may learn
Immortal gods from mortals to discern;
Lest, plung'd in drowsy Lethe's black abyss,
Some baneful dæmon keep my soul from bliss;
And lest deep merg'd in Hyle's stormy mire,
Her powers reluctant suffer tortures dire,
And some chill Fury with her freezing chain,
In ling'ring lethargy my life detain.
All-radiant governours of wisdom's light,
To me now hast'ning from the realms of night,
And ardent panting for the coasts of day,
Thro' sacred rites benignant point the way,
And mystic knowledge to my view disclose,
Since this for ever from your nature flows.

To VENUS*

A CELEBRATED royal fount I sing,
From foam begotten, and of Loves the spring,
Those winged, deathless powers, whose gen'ral sway
In diff'rent modes all mortal tribes obey.
With mental darts some pierce the god-like soul,
And freedom rouse unconscious of controul;
That anxious hence the centre to explore
Which lead on high from matter's stormy shore,
The ardent soul may meditate her flight,
And view their mother's palaces of light.
But others, watchful of their father's will,
Attend his councils and his laws fulfil,
His bounteous providence o'er all extend,
And strengthen generation without end.
And others last, the most inferior kind,
Preside o'er marriage, and its contracts bind,
Intent a race immortal to supply
From man calamitous and doom'd to die.
While all Cythera's high commands obey,
And bland attention to her labours pay.
O venerable goddess! hear my prayer,
For nought escapes thine universal ear:
Whether t' embrace the mighty heav'n is thine,
And fend the world from thence a soul divine;
Or whether, seated in th' ætherial plain,
Above these seven-fold starry orbs you reign,
Imparting to our ties, with bounteous mind,
A power untam'd, a vigour unconfin'd;—
Hear me, O goddess, and my life defend,

---

* For an account of this divinity, consult my notes on the Cratylus.

With labours fad, and anxious for their end;
Transfix my soul with darts of holy fire,
And far avert the flames of base desire.

To VENUS

THEE, Venus, royal Lycian queen, I sing,
To whom of old by deity inspir'd,
In grateful signal of thy fav'ring aid,
Our country's guides, a sacred temple rais'd
In Lycia; of the intellectual rites
Symbolical, which link'd in Hymen's bands
Celestial Venus and the god of fire.
Olympian hence they called thee, by whose power
They oft avoided death's destructive ire,
To virtue looking; and from fertile beds
Through thee, an offspring provident and strong
Rose into light; while all their days were crown'd.
With gentle peace, the source of tranquil bliss.
Illustrious queen! benignantly accept
The grateful tribute of this sacred hymn,
For we from Lycian blood derive our birth.
Expell base passions from my wand'ring soul,
And once more raise her to true beauty's light;
Averting far the irritation dire,
And rage insane, of earth-begotten love.

To MINERVA

DAUGHTER of ægis-bearing Jove, divine,
Propitious to thy vot'ries prayer incline;
From thy great father's fount supremely bright,
Like fire resounding, leaping into light.
Shield-bearing goddess, hear, to whom belong
A manly mind, and power to tame the strong!
Oh, sprung from matchless might, with joyful mind
Accept this hymn; benevolent and kind!
The holy gates of wisdom by thy hand
Are wide unfolded; and the daring band
Of earth-born giants, that in impious fight
Strove with thy sire, were vanquish'd by thy might.
Once by thy care, as sacred poets sing,
The heart of Bacchus, swiftly-slaughter'd king,
Was sav'd in æther, when, with fury fir'd,
The Titans fell against his life conspir'd;
And with relentless rage and thirst for gore,
Their hands his members into fragments tore:
But ever watchful of thy father's will,
Thy pow'r preferv'd him from succeeding ill,
Till from the secret counsels of his sire,
And born from Semele through heav'nly fire,
Great Dionysius to the world at length
Again appear'd with renovated strength.
Once, too, thy warlike axe, with matchless sway,
Lopp'd from their savage necks the heads away
Of furious beasts, and thus the pests destroy'd
Which long all-seeing Hecate annoy'd.
By thee benevolent great Juno's might
Was rous'd, to furnish mortals with delight:

And through life's wide and various range 'tis thine
Each part to beautify with arts divine:
Invigorated hence by thee, we find
A demiurgic impulse in the mind.
Towers proudly rais'd, and for protection strong,
To thee, dread guardian, deity belong,
As proper symbols of th' exalted height
Thy series claims amidst the courts of light.
Lands are belov'd by thee to learning prone,
And Athens, O Athena, is thy own!
Great goddess, hear! and on my dark'ned mind
Pour thy pure light in measure unconfin'd; —
That sacred light, O all-protecting queen,
Which beams eternal from thy face serene:
My soul, while wand'ring on the earth, inspire
With thy own blessed and impulsive fire;
And from thy fables, mystic and divine,
Give all her powers with holy light to shine.
Give love, give wisdom, and a power to love,
Incessant tending to the realms above;
Such as, unconscious of base earth's control,
Gently attracts the vice-subduing soul;
From night's dark region aids her to retire,
And once more gain the palace of her sire:
And if on me some just misfortune press,
Remove th' affliction, and thy suppliant bless.
All-saving goddess, to my prayer incline!
Nor let those horrid punishments be mine
Which guilty souls in Tartarus confine,
With fetters fast'ned to its brazen floors,
And lock'd by hell's tremendous iron doors.
Hear me, and save (for power is all thy own)
A soul desirous to be thine alone.

HYMNS
BY THE
TRANSLATOR

To CERES*

BOUNTEOUS Ceres, thee I sing,
Source of Jove the mighty king.
Goddess hail! of beauteous mien,
Splendid Rhea, Saturn's queen,
Gen'ral mother, nurse divine,
Nutriment to give is thine;
Food which first to gods extends,
And in sluggish body ends.
But the pure, immortal food,
Which supplies the gods with good,
From the beatific sight
Springs of beauty's perfect light;
Springs, when gods themselves desire.
And th' inferior view the higher.
Antient goddess, Saturn's wife,
Middle centre of all life,
Which for ever streams from thee.
All-prolific deity.
Juno, Vesta, ruling queen,
In thy vital fount are seen.
Juno, from whose fertile frame
Soul's self-motive, nature, came,
Whence its whole procession flows,
From thy right hand parts arose;

---

* According to Orpheus, as we are informed by Proclus on the Cratylus, this goddess, considered as united to Saturn, is called Rhea, and as producing Jupiter, Ceres: nor does this disagree with what Hesiod asserts in his Theogony, that Ceres is the daughter of Saturn; for considered as proceeding from her union with Saturn, to the production of Jupiter, she may be said to be the offspring of Saturn.

From thy left hand, Vesta bright,
Who wide scatters virtue's light.
Life not only, hence we see,
Springs, all-parent queen, from thee,
But life's bliss, fair virtue, streams
From thy fertile, mental beams:
And hence females offspring bear,
And from milky fountains rear.
Gracious goddess! may thy light
Beaming thro' Oblivion's night,
Fill my soul with food divine,
Which to give alone is thine;
Fill my soul with mental fire,
Perfect virtue, wing'd desire;
And from Hyle's stormy main,
To her father back again,
To her true immortal goal
Lead my wand'ring, weary soul,
Ardent panting to be blest,
In her native place of rest.

To JUPITER,
THE DEMIURGE OF THE WORLD

OF the mundane gods the king,
Mighty Jupiter, I sing;
Whose unenvying, perfect will,
Can the world with order fill,
And throughout with life inspire,
And expell confusion dire.
Pregnant with paternal power,
Shining like a fiery flower,
Jove at first, thro' æther bright,
Gave the world unhop'd-for light.
Jove all-seeing, Bromius strong,
Various names to thee belong.
Secret, mining, holy god,
Nature trembles at thy nod.
Father of this mighty whole,
Number, harmony, and soul,
Thee, Minerva's fire, I sing,
Saturn's son, of gods the king:
Light and spirit, Jove, are thine,
Council, intellect divine.
Mighty parent, may thine eye,
Which can every thought descry,
Piercing, swift, divinely bright,
Round me scatter mental light.
Oh regard my fervent prayer!
Free me from degrading care;
From the toil which want requires.
From the flames of base desires.
Dæmons from my life expel,

That in matter's darkness dwell;
Noxious to the human race,
Dogs of hell, terrific, base.
Fraudful Hyle here prepares
Me to plunge thro' magic snares,
Deep in black Barbaric mire,
Torn from thee, my lawful sire.
From dark uproar where she dwells,
Now she raises by her spells,
Tempests potent to control,
And in horror wrap the soul.
Place me in celestial light,
Far beyond this horrid night;
Far beyond her dire domain,
And oblivion's drowsy plain.
While, involv'd in earthly folds,
Me indignant Hyle holds,
While I struggle to be free,
Burst my bonds and fly to thee,
Strengthen me with mental might,
Wide my pinions stretch for flight,
That my soul may rapid rise,
And regain her native skies.
Now my fallen state I mourn,
Bodies scenes phantastic scorn,
Which the soul in evil hour
Subject to earth's sluggish power,
Till thro' thee her bonds she breaks,
And herself to life betakes.
With the luscious drink ensnar'd,
By Oblivion's hands prepar'd,
Staggering and oppress'd with sleep,
Thro' dark Hyle's stormy deep,
Headlong borne with forceful sway,

And, unconscious of the way,
Far I fell, midst dire uproar,
Till I touch'd this gloomy shore.
But my soul, now rous'd by thee,
And enabled truth to see,
Scorns her fetters, and aspires,
Borne on wings of pure desires,
To thy meadows full of light,
Fill'd with fountains of delight.
Arbiter of mental life,
Thro' these realms of endless strife,
Thro' earth's dark Tartarian tomb,
May thy light my steps illume;
And disclose the arduous way
To the coasts of mental day.
Cut the reins, and loose the bands,
Wove by guileful Nature's hands,
Which, forgetful of her birth,
Keep the soul a slave to earth.
From the fount contain'd in thee,
Source of life's prolific sea,
Here a mining drop I fell,
Destin'd here at times to dwell.
Oh restore me back again
From dark Hyle's stormy main,
From these realms of ceaseless strife,
To thy lucid fount of life;
To thy fount divinely pure,
Ever tranquil and secure.
Gracious bid my sorrows end,
And my exil'd soul defend;
Exil'd from her place of rest,
Wand'ring, weary, and opprest.
To thy bosom haste my flight,

Where e'en gods to dwell delight;
Where the soul from anxious toil
Rests, as in her native soil;
Finds the period of her woes,
Joy unmixt with sorrow knows;
And to be divinely free,
Loses all herself in thee.

To MINERVA

GREAT progeny of Jove, divinely bright,
Only-begotten source of mental light,
Whose beams the wise with vivid force inspire,
And leap resounding from a fount of fire,
Thee I invoke with supplicating voice,
Adore thy power, and in thy aid rejoyce:
To thee my wings from Hyle's stormy night
I stretch, impatient of a speedy flight;
For thee my soul far more than life desires,
And to thy light incessantly aspires.
By Vulcan's art thou fiercely sprung, 'tis said,
In splendid armour from thy father's head,
Shouting vehement, while with dire affright
Stood earth and heav'n astonished at the sight.
But this in symbols, obvious to the wise,
Thy amply-spreading government implies,
Which from the world's artificer extends,
And last in matter's lowest region ends;
While by the horror which thy wondrous birth
Produc'd at first in heav'n and mother earth,
Thy power exempt from mundane forms we learn,
And its occult prerogative discern.
Thy shouts too shew, that energy divine,
With efficacious vigour fraught, is thine.
Thy dreadful shield, in mystic fables fam'd,
Occultly signifies the power untam'd
Which in thy essence first appears, and thence
Becomes the gods' invincible defence;
Thro' which from passion they remain secure,
And reign triumphant and divinely pure.

Thy spear, of all-pervading power's the sign,
(For nought can e'er thy matchless might confine)
Thro' which the gods, unconscious of control,
Pass without contact, thro' this mighty whole
Forms sublunary aid, and in their course
Base matter amputate with vig'rous force.
Hail, blue-ey'd maid, of countenance serene!
Who reign'st in heav'n apparent and unseen,
And thence, through Hyle's realms, involv'd in storms,
Pourst in abundant streams resplendent forms.
To thee triumphant, and of bounteous mind,
The ram celestial is by lot assign'd,
And equinoctial circle, where resides
A motive power that o'er the world presides.
Victorious virgin, may thy vivid light
Disperse the mists produc'd by Lethe's night,
My soul from earth's impurities refine,
And all her pow'rs expand through rites divine;
That wing'd and ardent with celestial fire,
She soon may gain the palace of her sire,
And there once more may rest from anxious toil,
Fix'd in her long-deserted native soil.

To VESTA

SATURN'S daughter, antient dame,
Seat of fire's unweary'd frame,
Source of virtue's perfect light,
Juno's equal, Vesta bright,
Stable goddess, essence fair,
Gracious listen to my prayer;
And while ardent thee I sing,
Borne on pure devotion's wing,
With thy unpolluted fire
All my mental powers inspire.
From the gods by men divine
Liberated called, 'tis thine
Essence to illumine pure,
Uniform, unchang'd, and sure.
Hence the mundane gods we see,
Through thy stable deity,
Firmly in themselves abide,
And immutably preside
O'er the fluctuating forms,
O'er the dire resounding storms,
Of dark Hyle's rolling main,
Barren, impotent, and vain.
Thy abiding splendours hence
Firm stability dispense,
To the axis and the poles,
Round which heav'n incessant rolls;
And to earth's all-flow'ry frame,
Earth, prolific, central dame!
Blessed goddess, may thy light,
Beaming far thro' Lethe's night,

Widely featuring virtue's fires,
Fill my soul with pure desires;
And disclose the arduous way
To the courts of mental day.
To thy stable, shining seat,
Wisdom's undisturb'd retreat,
Harbour of deific rest
To the wand'ring and opprest.
While on Hyle's stormy sea,
Wide I roam in search of thee,
Graciously thine arm extend,
And my soul from ill defend:
Gracious bid my sorrows cease;
Crown my future days with peace,
With the splendid gifts of health,
With the bliss of needful wealth;
And soon cut the fatal folds,
Through which guileful nature holds
Me indignant from thy sight,
Exil'd in the realms of night,
From my father's bosom torn,
Wand'ring, weary and forlorn,
That my soul with rapid wing,
From Oblivion's coast may spring,
May once more triumphant gain
Truth's immortal, shining plain,
And in her conceal'd abodes
Ravish'd view the god of gods.

To MERCURY

HERMES I sing, a god supremely bright,
Who first emerging from Jove's fount of light,
Upborne on beauteous wings, from thence descends,
Till last his lucid course in Hades ends.
Angel of Jove, unfolding truth divine,
Propitious to thy vot'ry's prayer incline,
And while to thee my suppliant voice I raise,
Accept, well pleas'd, this tribute of my praise.
By antient bards, in mystic verse 'tis sung,
That thou, great god, from prudent Maia sprung:
But this in symbols, obvious to the wise,
Thy nature with invention fraught implies;
Since *search*, which into light *invention* leads,
First from fair Maia secretly proceeds,
And as unfolding mighty Jove's decree,
Mathesis owes its origin to thee;
Hence fallen souls, to deep research inclin'd,
By thee inspir'd, eternal truth may find;
When rous'd by discipline from Lethe's night,
They raise their eyes to intellectual light.
To thee unnumber'd benefits we owe;
From thee gymnastic, music, reasoning flow.
Hence thro' the first with vigor we inspire
In youth, the languid nature of desire;
And anger, merg'd in matter's gloomy deep,
Wake into energy from death-like sleep;
While thro' the power of melody divine
We force e'en rage its fury to resign.
And last, the seeds of truth in dormant state,
The vivid wings of reas'ning suscitate:

Hence, as of harmony the mighty sire,
The wise ador'd thee as the starry lyre,
Whose strains wide-spreading thro' the azure round,
The gods transport with deifying sound,
And even in the dark Tartarian gulf rebound.
And as 'tis thine o'er learning to preside,
The wise invok'd thee, as of souls the guide,
Who leadst them upwards to the splendid plain
Of sacred truth, from Hyle's dire domain,
Oblivion's sleep expelling from their sight,
And wide-expanding recollection's light.
All bounteous Hermes, hear my fervent prayer,
And make my future life thy constant care,
Teach me what rites th' offended gods may please,
And what the means their anger to appease:
For long thro' marine and material foes,
My soul has suffer'd complicated woes;
And all her efforts have as yet been vain
T' escape the fury of the avenging main.
Come, gracious god, thy saving arm extend,
And from her natal ills my soul defend;
Urge all her powers by baneful night oppress'd
To rise victorious to the goal of rest;
The splendid goal of loud-resounding fire,
And all-attractive centre of desire;
That wing'd and ardent, and from guilt refin'd,
She thus the end of all her woes may find.

THE END

Printed in Great Britain
by Amazon